For All my friends at Londonderry
With lots of love
Bob [signature]
xxx

A Little Boy In The Land Of Rhyme

A Book of Simple Wonder

by Bo Lozoff

Book design and illustrations by Deborah Hayner

For Wyatt, and a Wonder-filled Life

www.rockingmonkey.com

Signature Book Printing, Inc., www.sbpbooks.com,
First Printing April 2011, Printed in U.S.A.
ISBN: 978-0-578-07810-6

© Copyright 2011 Bo Lozoff. All rights reserved.

Once upon a time,

There was a little boy

In the Land of Rhyme...

He woke one morning,

Rubbed the sleep from

his eyes,

And heard two bluebirds

Discussing the sky.

Most people think

We can't understand birds,

But a mind that is pure

Can hear much more than words.

One bluebird said,

Sky is five miles high!

But the other said,

No, we're already in the sky.

Then the little boy sat on his front steps to wonder:

And if the other bird's right,

And they're already there,

Then where does sky stop,

Where, oh where?

And when I watch an ant carry a crumb of bread,

Does he think the sky

Is all around my head?

And do the tiny living things

In the soil of a plant

Think that the sky

Is all around the ant?

Then his daddy came out

Because he overheard.

And said, son, the answer is

that sky's just a word.

It means all the space

That seems up so far:

And where it starts and stops

Depends on where you are!

Rain

Then they both watched the sky

'Til it started to rain

And the little boy listened

To his daddy explain...

How the clouds gather mist

From the sea and the sky

And the mist turns to water

As it cools way up high.

Then the clouds get heavy,

And big all around

'Til they drop all the water

As rain to the ground.

And the rain goes to water

The plants and the trees.

And fills up the rivers,

And even the seas.

And cools off the sidewalks

And gets kids all wet,

And leaves beautiful rainbows

You'll never forget!

And it washes the birds,

And the goats and the sheep,

And the hills and the valleys

And the mountains so steep

And cleans up the sky

So that it can stay blue

And washes our house,

And your bicycle, too.

Rain helps everything grow,

Even you, even me,

Then flows back through the earth

To its home in the sea.

Sea

The little boy listened,

And then asked thoughtfully,

But tell me, Daddy,

What is the sea?

The sea is the mother

Of all that's alive.

Without the sea,

Our planet just couldn't survive.

Long before anything

Walked on the earth

Mother Sea had already

Given birth...

To plants and fishes

That played in the tide...

And the little boy listened,

With his eyes opened wide.

The sea is a living and

Breathing thing.

Put a shell to your ear

And you'll hear the sea sing!

So the little boy did,

And he shouted with glee

Daddy, oh Daddy,

It's really the sea!

Then his daddy said,

Yes, and I'll tell you what's more:

We all feel at home

By the sea and its shore.

As if a lifetime

Back in everyone's past

Was spent as a sailing-man

Under the mast.

There's more sea than land,

More than twice as much

When you count all the oceans

And rivers and such.

And the sea and the land,

And all they embrace

We've come to call Earth,

Our planet in space.

Earth

Then the little boy

took a walk with his dad

And they talked about

All that our Planet Earth had,

Such as tigers and movies

And holes in the ground

And forests and stop signs,

And hills to slide down...

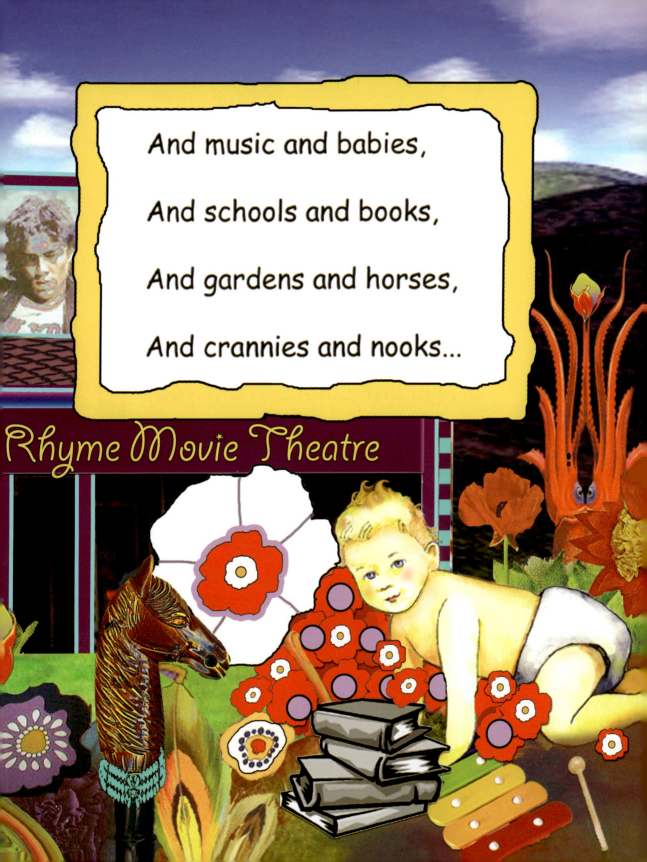

And people with skin

Different colors from you,

And people who speak

Other languages, too.

But the little boy's mind

Was in some other place.

For he just couldn't picture

Where the Earth is in space.

Or even what was meant

By a planet as such,

And with so many planets,

Why they never touch.

So he asked his dad

To explain it to him,

And they sat by a pond

On a log at the rim.

Son, the Earth is a tiny

grain of sand.

And all of space is but

The palm of God's Hand.

Everything's big, and

Everything's small

When you think of the atom

On up to the All.

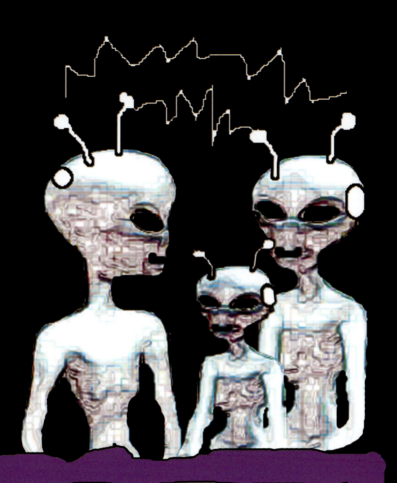

There may be life on

Other planets as well.

But nobody knows,

Only time will tell.

Time

Then they walked into the woods

Full of maple leaves falling

And his daddy said,

That means Autumn's come calling.

And Autumn is a time,

Just like summer, winter, spring;

And nature always tries

To be in time with everything.

His daddy said, well son,

No one really knows.

We can't touch it or taste it,

Or watch where it goes.

All we do is measure it

In many different ways,

And name them seconds, minutes,

Hours, weeks, months, days...

And seasons and years,

And phases of the moon,

And now and then,

And later and soon.

No matter what you're doing,

You're also spending time.

And you can't replace it

Like you can a nickel or a dime.

Time is not a "What" or "Where,"

Time is just a "When."

And when a minute's over,

That minute never comes again.

The whole earth moves through Time

Just as it moves through space.

And a land where Time does not exist--

Well, you can't imagine such a place.

The Little boy said,

Gosh Daddy, Time sounds really odd!

Prayer

Now the little boy was awed

By all these wondrous things...

He loved his Dad, he loved his Mom,

He loved the birds that sing...

He loved the sky, the rain, the sea,

The Earth and Father Time,

And all the people that he knew

In the Land of Rhyme.

He ran, he jumped, he hugged a tree,

He turned a quick cartwheel,

He threw his arms out to the sky,

Let out a happy squeal.

He felt so good, he felt so pure,

He felt so deeply clean.

Then his dad caught up and said, son,

That's the nicest prayer I've ever seen.

The boy said but I didn't pray!

And his dad said oh, you're wrong.

You prayed as much as ever,

And every bit as strong.

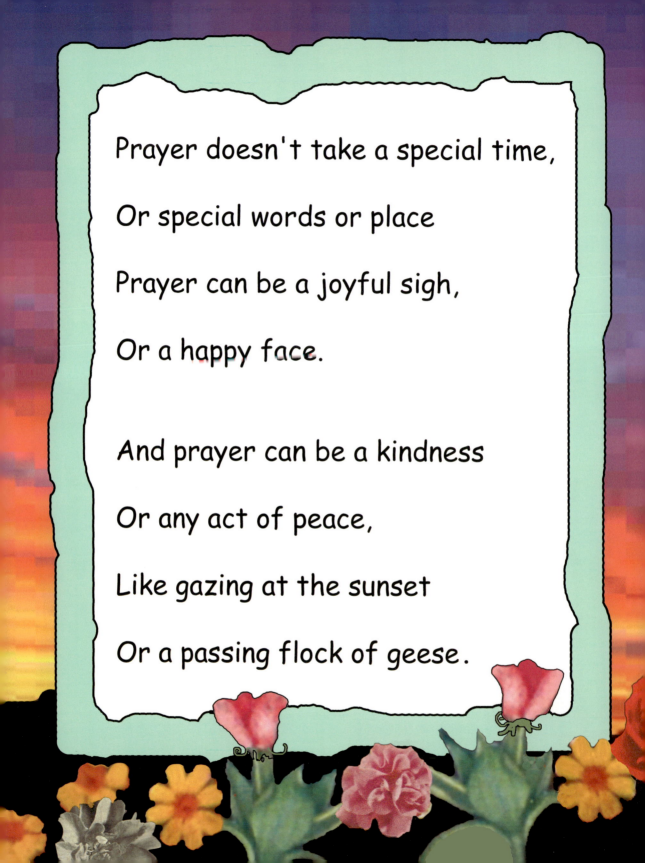

Prayer doesn't take a special time,

Or special words or place

Prayer can be a joyful sigh,

Or a happy face.

And prayer can be a kindness

Or any act of peace,

Like gazing at the sunset

Or a passing flock of geese.

Many people pray

In many different ways,

But the little boy lived his prayer,

Each and every day.

So the boy and his daddy

Walked in silence for awhile

And thought about their lovely day.

And preserved it with a smile.

Bo Lozoff is a teacher, author, and singer-songwriter whose work has drawn fans as diverse as His Holiness the Dalai Lama and Mister Rogers, who called Bo one of his "personal heroes." The Utne Reader has named Bo Lozoff "one of America's 100 spiritual visionaries." Bo's first book, We're All Doing Time (1984), has been hailed by the Village Voice as "one of the ten books everyone in the world should read." Bo and his wife, Sita, have received numerous humanitarian awards for their groundbreaking work with prisoners and prison staff throughout the world. In 1999, Bo was awarded an honorary doctorate from Chicago Theological Seminary.

This is Dr. Lozoff's second publication for children, the first being The Wonderful Life of a Fly Who Couldn't Fly, published in 2002 by Hampton Roads, and distributed now, along with all Bo's books, CDs, and DVDs, by Human Kindness Foundation (**www.humankindness.org**). Bo actually wrote A Little Boy in the Land of Rhyme at the age of 23, in 1970, while Sita was pregnant with their son Joshua Lozoff, now an acclaimed magician in his own right (**www.deep-magic.com**). Not a word has been changed since then. This is its first publication.

Deborah Hayner is an artist living and working in San Francisco, whose studio is located at Hunters Point Shipyard. Born in San Francisco in 1952, Ms. Hayner studied at the Academy of Art. Her work is experimental and includes found object assemblage, mixed media collage and painting, digital photo manipulations, altered books, art to wear, and installations. She exhibits her work regularly, participating in both local and national fine art exhibitions. Ms. Hayner has collaborated on several children's books, including internationally published and translated "Dream Song of the Eagle" by Ted Andrews. To learn more about this artist visit (**www.haynerart.com**).